BAKES

that

BREAK

the

INTERNET

BAKES
that
BREAK
the
INTERNET

Kat Buckley
@thebakingexplorer

All the Trending Bakes from Faultline Cakes to Freakshakes!

POP PRESS

CAKES & CUPCAKES

8

COOKIES

36

NO-BAKE TREATS

60

TRAYBAKES

78

DESSERTS

100

Introduction

Hi, I'm Kat! My adventure into the world of baking began in 2012, when I started my blog The Baking Explorer. What began as a hobby, quickly turned into a passion. I wanted to make every cake and learn every technique I discovered. Over the years I have taught myself how to bake and running my blog is now my full-time job. I absolutely love how baking can bring people together and lift their mood. Sharing delicious food with others is one of life's simple pleasures.

If you're a regular on social media, you'll notice everyone loves a good food craze. I created the recipes in this book, after being inspired by the most popular bakes and tastes that the internet has been drooling over. Although this book is called *Bakes That Break The Internet*, I don't think any of the treats featured are at risk of going out of fashion. They may have had their viral moments, but they are still some of the most delicious bakes and classic flavours around.

This book contains 40 delicious bakes for every occasion, from Anti-Gravity Chocolate Cake for an impressive birthday treat to Coffee Mug Cake for when you're in the mood for something quick and easy. For a gooey chocolate fix, get a batch of Black Forest Brownies in the oven and for enjoying with a cup of tea, you can't go wrong with the Cookie Dippers.

I hope you enjoy baking from this book. I'd love to see what you make, so please tag me on social media @thebakingexplorer and share your photos using #BakesThatBreakTheInternet.

TIP
You don't need a stand mixer for these recipes, you can use a handheld electric whisk, or for many you can mix by hand. It might take longer, but the results are just as delicious!

CAKES
CUP

& CAKES

Custard Cream Fault Line Cake

Fault line cakes are showstopping cakes featuring a 'crack' all around the middle, showcasing their theme or flavour. The edges of the crack are painted with edible gold paint to make the design even more eye-catching! I've chosen custard creams for this bake as they are such a tasty favourite which have stood the test of time. This cake is filled with vanilla buttercream and a homemade custard for lots of sweet vanilla flavour. If you're wanting to impress, then this is the cake to make!

Prep time: 25 minutes
Bake time: 35–40 minutes
Chill time: 1 hour
Decorating time: 1 hour
Serves: 16+

500g baking spread, softened, plus extra for greasing
500g caster sugar
9 large eggs
3 tsp vanilla extract
500g self-raising flour

FOR THE FILLING
165ml whole milk
¼ tsp vanilla extract or paste
2 egg yolks
45g caster sugar
15g cornflour

FOR THE BUTTERCREAM
700g unsalted butter, softened
1.4kg icing sugar
3 tsp vanilla extract
5 tbsp milk
4 tsp white food colouring (optional – I use Wilton)

Preheat the oven to 150°C fan/Gas Mark 3½ and grease and line three 20cm cake tins at least 5cm deep.

For the cake, mix together the baking spread and sugar, ideally using a stand mixer with the paddle attachment, or an electric hand mixer, for 3 minutes until smooth and fluffy. Add the eggs and vanilla extract and whisk well until combined. Gently whisk or fold in the flour. Divide the cake batter between the cake tins, using scales for accuracy if you like. Bake for 35–40 minutes, or until risen, golden and a skewer inserted into the centre of each cake comes out clean. Leave the cakes to cool completely, either in the tins, or remove them from the tins and place on wire racks.

To make the custard filling, heat the milk with the vanilla extract or paste in a pan on a low heat until the milk starts steaming. While the milk mixture is heating up, whisk the egg yolks and sugar together in a mixing bowl until the mixture thickens and turns paler in colour. Then add the cornflour and mix it in. Pour the hot milk mixture into the egg yolk mixture slowly, whisking continuously. Once they are combined, return the mixture to the pan on a medium heat. Stir the mixture constantly as it heats up and starts to thicken.

Recipe continues overleaf

FOR DECORATION

400g custard cream
    biscuits
1 tsp edible gold lustre
    dust (I used Sugarflair
    Antique Gold)
2–3 tsp dipping solution
    (or vodka)

Once the mixture has thickened, remove it from the heat. Put it into a bowl and cover it with clingfilm so that the clingfilm directly touches the top of the custard. Transfer to the fridge to cool completely. If there are any lumps in the custard, you can push it through a fine sieve once it has cooled.

To make the buttercream, mix the butter on its own for a few minutes. Add the icing sugar, vanilla extract, milk and white food colouring (if using) and mix until smooth. For the best results, use an electric hand whisk or a stand mixer with the paddle attachment. If your buttercream is too stiff, you can add a little more milk to loosen it.

Level off each cake with a cake leveller or knife so they have flat tops. Place the first cake layer onto a cake board. To make it easier to decorate, place the cake board onto a decorating turntable with a non-slip mat between the board and the turntable. Spread a thin layer of the buttercream over the first layer of cake, then pipe a ring of buttercream all around the edge of the cake using a piping bag fitted with a round nozzle. Fill the middle of the cake with half of the custard. Add the second cake layer, repeat this same process, then add the third and final cake layer. Cover the whole cake in a thin layer of buttercream (a crumb coat), then stick custard cream biscuits all around the middle of the cake. Cut some of them in half. Chill the cake in the fridge for 30 minutes to set the buttercream.

Cover the cake in a thicker layer of buttercream, slightly cover the edges of the custard cream biscuits on either side but keep the majority of the biscuits uncovered. Use a buttercream scraper tool to smooth out the buttercream. Pop it back in the fridge for 30 minutes.

Mix the lustre dust and dipping solution together. Paint the edges of the buttercream gold around the custard cream biscuits using a small clean paintbrush. Using a piping bag fitted with a nozzle (I used a Wilton 2D), pipe the remaining buttercream on top of the cake in swirls, and decorate with the remaining custard cream biscuits. Serve immediately. The biscuits will go soft the longer they are in contact with the buttercream. Store any leftovers in an airtight container in the fridge for up to 3 days. The cake needs to be kept in the fridge due to the custard filling, but I recommend bringing it back to room temperature before eating.

Rainbow Cupcakes

These bright and colourful treats are so fun and attractive! Each rainbow cupcake is topped with 'clouds' of soft whipped cream, fluffy marshmallows and 'gold coin' sprinkles. I recommend using professional-grade food colouring for the best and brightest results.

Prep time: 35 minutes
Bake time: 25–30 minutes
Decorating time: 20 minutes
Makes: 12

200g baking spread, softened
200g caster sugar
3 large eggs
1 tbsp milk
1 tsp vanilla extract
200g self-raising flour
Red, yellow, orange, green, blue and purple food colouring (I use Sugarflair)

FOR THE TOPPING
300ml double cream
1 tbsp icing sugar
1 tsp vanilla extract
50g white mini marshmallows (gelatine-free if serving to vegetarians)
Gold coin sprinkles

Preheat the oven to 140°C fan/Gas Mark 3, and line a 12-hole cupcake tin with cupcake cases.

For the cupcake sponge, mix together the baking spread and sugar, ideally using a stand mixer with the paddle attachment, or an electric hand mixer, for exactly 5 minutes until smooth and fluffy. Add the eggs, milk and vanilla extract and whisk well until combined. Gently whisk or fold in the flour. Divide the cupcake mixture equally between six bowls (I got roughly 130g mixture per bowl). Add a different food colouring to each bowl.

Place spoonfuls of each colour of mixture one at a time in the cupcake cases, making sure each cupcake case gets a bit of every colour. Repeat until all of the mixture is used up. Bake the cupcakes for 25–30 minutes or until a thin skewer inserted into the centre comes out clean. Remove the cupcakes from the tin and transfer them to a wire rack to cool completely.

Whip the double cream with the icing sugar and vanilla extract until thick. This can be done with a hand whisk and some elbow grease, or for a quick and less tiring option, use a stand mixer with the whisk attachment. Transfer the whipped cream to a piping bag fitted with the nozzle of your choice, and pipe swirls onto each cupcake, or you can dollop it on with a spoon. Decorate with the mini marshmallows and gold sprinkles. Serve immediately. Store any leftovers in the fridge and eat within 2 days.

TIP
If you prefer buttercream to whipped cream, use the recipe from Filled Sweetie Cupcakes on page 27, without the food colouring.

Cakes & Cupcakes

Ice Cream Cone Cupcakes

Prep time: 20 minutes
Bake time: 20 minutes
Decorating time: 20 minutes
Makes: 12

12 flat-bottomed ice-cream cones (I use Askeys)
135g baking spread, softened
135g caster sugar
2 large eggs
1 tbsp milk
1 tsp vanilla extract
135g self-raising flour

FOR THE BUTTERCREAM
175g unsalted butter, softened
350g icing sugar
1 tsp vanilla extract
1 tbsp milk

FOR DECORATION
4 chocolate flake bars, cut into thirds
Sprinkles

These cute treats are a great way to surprise your guests. Instead of ice cream, they'll bite into smooth vanilla buttercream and a hidden cake centre! They're perfect for your summertime get togethers, and kids will absolutely love both decorating and eating them.

Preheat the oven to 160°C fan/Gas Mark 4. Cut out strips of foil and wrap them around the ice cream cones; you don't need to cover the bottom with foil. Place them in a 12-hole cupcake tin.

For the cupcake sponge, mix together the baking spread and sugar, ideally using a stand mixer with the paddle attachment, or an electric hand mixer, for 2–3 minutes until smooth and fluffy. Add the eggs, milk and vanilla extract and whisk well. Gently whisk or fold in the flour. Divide the mixture between the 12 cones and bake for 25 minutes, or until they are golden brown, and a thin skewer inserted into the centre of each cake comes out clean. Carefully remove the foil wraps and transfer the cupcakes to a wire rack to cool completely.

For the buttercream, mix the butter on its own for a few minutes. Add the icing sugar, vanilla extract and milk and mix until smooth. For the best results, use an electric hand whisk or stand mixer with the paddle attachment. If your buttercream is too stiff, you can add a little more milk to loosen it. Pipe the buttercream onto each cupcake using a piping bag fitted with a nozzle of your choice, or spread it on with a spoon. Insert a third of a chocolate flake bar into each one and add your choice of sprinkles. Store in an airtight container in a cool place and eat within 3 days.

Easter Chocolate Cupcakes

Whether Easter is on its way, or you've got leftover Easter chocolate to use up, you can't go wrong with these delicious cupcakes. This is an easy recipe for anyone to make, and the buttercream is piped like a nest so that three little chocolate eggs can fit snuggly in the centre.

Prep time: 25 minutes
Bake time: 25–30 minutes
Decorating time: 20 minutes
Makes: 12

175g baking spread, softened
175g caster sugar
3 large eggs
2 tbsp milk
150g self-raising flour
25g cocoa powder
¼ tsp baking powder

FOR THE BUTTERCREAM
200g unsalted butter, softened
350g icing sugar
50g cocoa powder
3 tbsp milk

FOR DECORATION
36 small chocolate eggs (120g – I use Mini Eggs)

Preheat the oven to 140°C fan/Gas Mark 3 and line a 12-hole cupcake tin with cupcake cases.

For the cupcake sponge, mix together the baking spread and sugar, ideally using a stand mixer with the paddle attachment, or an electric hand mixer, for exactly 5 minutes until smooth and fluffy. Add the eggs and milk and whisk them in well until combined. Gently whisk or fold in the flour, cocoa powder and baking powder. Divide the mixture equally between the cupcake cases and bake for 25–30 minutes or until a thin skewer inserted into the centre of the cupcakes comes out clean. Remove the cupcakes from the tin and put them on a wire rack to cool completely.

For the buttercream, mix the butter on its own for a few minutes. Add the icing sugar, cocoa powder and milk and mix until smooth. For the best results, use an electric hand mixer or a stand mixer with the paddle attachment. If your buttercream is too stiff, you can add a little more milk to loosen it. Spread or pipe the buttercream on top of the cupcakes. To make the nest shape, pipe a flat swirl, then pipe a circle of buttercream only around the edge of the flat swirl, leaving a hole in the centre. Or dollop some buttercream on top with a spoon, smooth it out, then scoop a dip out of the centre. Fill the hole in the centre with three chocolate eggs per cupcake. Store in an airtight container in a cool place and eat within 3 days.

TIP
You can make these cupcakes any time of year and customise them with your favourite chocolates or sweets, depending on the occasion!

Anti-Gravity Chocolate Cake

This showstopping cake defies the laws of gravity and creates the illusion that sweets are pouring out of a sweetie bag and flooding the cake. The effect is easier to create than you may think, and it involves a straw, a skewer and some sticky tape. A little patience is required when it comes to creating the stream of pouring sweets, but it is so worth it for this impressive trick. The cake itself is a moist chocolate cake that's sure to be a hit with any audience.

Prep time: 45 minutes
Bake time: 25 minutes
Decorating time: 1 hour
Serves: 16

235g baking spread, softened
235g caster sugar
4 large eggs
200g self-raising flour
35g cocoa powder
¼ tsp baking powder

FOR THE BUTTERCREAM
175g unsalted butter, softened
300g icing sugar
40g cocoa powder
2–3 tbsp milk

FOR DECORATION
Chocolate finger biscuits (I use Cadbury Fingers)
1 wooden skewer
1 paper straw
1 sweet bag
25g milk chocolate, melted
400g sugar-coated chocolates

Preheat the oven to 150°C fan/Gas mark 3½ and grease and line two 20cm cake tins at least 5cm deep.

For the cake, mix together the baking spread and sugar, ideally using a stand mixer with the paddle attachment, or an electric hand mixer, for 3–5 minutes until smooth and fluffy. Add the eggs and whisk well until combined. Gently whisk or fold in the flour, cocoa powder and baking powder. Divide the cake batter between the cake tins, using scales for accuracy if you like. Bake for 20–25 minutes, or until risen and a thin skewer inserted into the centre of each cake comes out clean. Leave the cakes to cool completely, either in the tins, or transfer them to a wire rack.

For the buttercream, mix the butter on its own for a few minutes. Add the icing sugar, cocoa powder and milk, and mix until smooth. For the best results, use an electric hand whisk or stand mixer with the paddle attachment. If your buttercream is too stiff, you can add a little more milk to loosen it.

Put the first layer of cake onto a cake board and spread a layer of buttercream over it, then top with the second cake layer. Spread an even layer of buttercream around the sides of the cake, then stick the chocolate finger biscuits to it while the buttercream is still wet. Push the skewer into the centre of the cake.

Cakes & Cupcakes

Recipe continues overleaf   21

Place the straw over it and bend the straw about 3cm from the top. If the skewer is too long to allow this, trim it to size. Use some sticky tape to attach a sweet bag to the bent part of the straw.

Use the melted milk chocolate to stick the sugar-coated chocolates to the straw. Start at the bottom and work your way up. You may need to pop the cake in the fridge between each layer of sweets to allow the chocolate to harden. Or if you have some spray ice, you can use that to set the chocolate. Keep going all the way to the top of the straw and slightly into the sweet bag. Cover the top of the cake with the remaining buttercream, and top with the remaining sugar-coated chocolates. Store any leftovers in an airtight container in a cool place and eat within 3 days.

TIP

You can use any kind of sweets for this cake, or a mixture of sweets and chocolates.

Speculoos Drip Cake

This cake is the ultimate speculoos showstopper! It's made up of three layers of brown sugar and speculoos cake, filled and covered with speculoos buttercream and decorated with a speculoos spread drip and speculoos biscuits. It's basically speculoos heaven! It would be such a perfect cake for any fan of speculoos on their birthday – or any other celebration.

Prep time: 1 hour
Bake time: 35–40 minutes
Chill time: 1 hour and 30 minutes
Decorating time: 1 hour
Serves: 16+

485g baking spread, softened, plus extra for greasing
485g soft light brown sugar
225g speculoos spread, smooth (I use Biscoff)
9 large eggs
1½ tbsp milk
485g self-raising flour

FOR THE BUTTERCREAM
500g unsalted butter, softened
1kg icing sugar
400g smooth speculoos spread (I use Biscoff)
3–4 tbsp milk

FOR DECORATION
135g smooth speculoos spread (I use Biscoff)
16 speculoos biscuits (I use Biscoff)

Preheat the oven to 150°C fan/Gas Mark 3½ and grease and line three 20cm cake tins at least 5cm deep.

For the sponge, in a large bowl, mix together the baking spread and sugar for about 3–5 minutes until fluffy, ideally using a stand mixer with the paddle attachment, or an electric hand mixer. Mix in the speculoos spread. Add the eggs and milk and whisk until fully incorporated. Gently whisk or fold in the flour. Divide the mixture between the tins, using scales for accuracy if you like. Bake for 35–40 minutes or until a thin skewer inserted into the middle comes out clean. Leave the sponges to fully cool either in the tins or remove from the tins and place on wire racks

For the buttercream, mix the butter on its own for a few minutes. Add the icing sugar, speculoos spread and milk and mix until smooth. For the best results, use an electric hand whisk or stand mixer with the paddle attachment. If your buttercream is too stiff, you can add a little more milk to loosen it.

If the cakes have domed on top, level them off with a cake leveller or a knife. To decorate, place the first cake layer onto a cake board. To make it easier to decorate, place the cake board onto a decorating turntable with a non-slip mat between the board and the turntable.

Recipe continues overleaf

Cakes & Cupcakes

Spread or pipe buttercream over the first cake layer, then add the second cake layer, spread more buttercream over that, then add the third and final cake layer on top. Cover the whole cake with a base layer of buttercream (a crumb coat) and smooth it out. Chill in the fridge for 30 minutes to firm up.

Coat the cake with a second and thicker layer of buttercream and smooth it out as best you can, using a buttercream scraper tool. Put it back in the fridge for 30 minutes to set.

Melt the speculoos for the drip in the microwave for just 20 seconds, or until it's a pourable consistency. Transfer it to a piping bag or a squeezy bottle, or you can use a spoon. Pipe the speculoos spread around the edge of the cake, allowing it to drip down the sides in varying amounts. Once the drips are complete, cover the whole top of the cake with the remaining speculoos spread. Use a palette knife or the back of a spoon to smooth it out. Put the cake in the fridge for 30 minutes for the speculoos to firm up.

Put the remaining buttercream into a piping bag fitted with your chosen nozzle and pipe swirls all around the edge of the cake. To decorate with speculoos biscuits, snap about a third of each biscuit off and insert the remaining larger pieces of biscuit vertically between the buttercream swirls. Crush the smaller pieces of biscuit into crumbs and decorate the centre of the cake with them. The biscuits will become softer after being in contact with the buttercream, so do this as close to serving the cake as you can. Any leftovers will keep in an airtight container in a cool place for 3 days.

Filled Sweetie Cupcakes

These colourful and attractive cupcakes hide a delicious secret. Inside each one is a filling of luscious chocolate hazelnut spread. You can choose to let your friends and family in on the hidden surprise, or let them discover it for themselves as they bite into these fun cupcakes!

Prep time: 25 minutes
Bake time: 25–30 minutes
Decorating time: 25 minutes
Makes: 12

175g baking spread, softened
175g caster sugar
3 large eggs
1 tsp vanilla extract
175g self-raising flour

FOR THE FILLING
150g chocolate hazelnut spread, warmed for 25 seconds in the microwave (I use Nutella)

FOR THE BUTTERCREAM
175g unsalted butter, softened
300g icing sugar
2 tsp vanilla extract
3 drops of pink food colouring (I use Pro Gel)
2 tbsp milk

FOR DECORATION
Dolly mixture
Jelly beans
Jelly tots
Sprinkles

Preheat the oven to 140°C fan/Gas Mark 3 and line a 12-hole cupcake tin with cupcake cases.

For the cupcake sponge, mix together the baking spread and sugar, ideally using a stand mixer with the paddle attachment, or an electric hand mixer, for exactly 5 minutes until smooth and fluffy. Add the eggs and vanilla extract and whisk them in until combined. Gently whisk or fold in the flour. Divide the mixture equally between the cupcake cases and bake them for 25–30 minutes or until a thin skewer inserted into the centre of the cupcakes comes out clean. Remove the cupcakes from the tin and transfer them to a wire rack to cool completely.

Use a cupcake corer, an apple corer or a knife to make a hole in each cupcake. Fill with the warmed chocolate hazelnut spread.

For the buttercream, mix the butter on its own for a few minutes. Add the icing sugar, vanilla extract, pink food colouring and milk and mix until smooth. For the best results, use an electric hand whisk or stand mixer with the paddle attachment. If your buttercream is too stiff, you can add a little more milk to loosen it. Spread or pipe the buttercream on top of the cupcakes. Decorate with the sweets and sprinkles. Store in an airtight container in a cool place and eat within 3 days.

TIP
You can fill these cupcakes with a variety of delicious surprises, such as lemon curd, speculoos spread, any flavour of jam, caramel sauce, etc.

Cakes & Cupcakes

Rainbow Cake Jars

It does not get more showstopping than these epic Rainbow Cake Jars! Cake jars are a brilliant way of displaying the yummy insides of a sponge, and they're also a handy way to transport cake without damaging it. I've gone all out with the decoration for a stunning party-ready effect, but you can enjoy these cake jars on the go too, with a simpler design.

Prep time: 45 minutes
Bake time: 15 minutes
Decorating time: 1 hour
Makes: 5

450g baking spread, softened, plus extra for greasing
450g caster sugar
6 medium eggs
1½ tsp vanilla extract
450g self-raising flour
Red, orange, yellow, green, blue and purple food colouring (I use Sugarflair)

FOR THE BUTTERCREAM
550g unsalted butter, softened
1.1kg icing sugar
3 tsp vanilla extract
3–4 tbsp milk
White food colouring (optional – I use Wilton)

Before you start: Each colour cake is made in a 20cm round cake tin. Depending on how many tins of this size you own, you can make several of the sponges at once, or one at a time. Each sponge requires 75g baking spread, 75g caster sugar, 1 egg, ¼ teaspoon of vanilla extract, 75g self-raising flour and the relevant food colouring. Do not make lots of cake mixture and leave it out on a work surface, as it needs to go into the oven shortly after making it. You will also need 6 x 500ml jars, 7cm wide and 15cm tall, or if you want to make fewer layers/colours, you can use shorter jars.

Preheat the oven to 150°C fan/Gas mark 3½ and grease and line your 20cm cake tin(s).

Mix together the baking spread and caster sugar, ideally using a stand mixer with the paddle attachment or an electric hand mixer, for 3 minutes until smooth and fluffy. Add the egg(s) and vanilla extract and whisk them in well until combined. Gently whisk or fold in the flour. If you're making several of the colours at once, split the cake batter equally into bowls at this stage. Add the relevant food colourings and mix them in until you have a bright shade. Add the cake batter to the tin(s) and spread out into an even layer. Bake for 15 minutes or until a thin skewer inserted into the centre comes out clean. Put on a wire rack to cool completely.

Recipe continues overleaf

Cakes & Cupcakes

FOR DECORATION
(optional)
25g sprinkles
50g white modelling paste
   (or white fondant)
2 tsp edible gold lustre dust
   (I use Sugarflair Antique
   Gold)
3–4 tsp dipping solution
   (or vodka)
¼ tsp edible glitter
50g white chocolate
25ml double cream
40g white candy melts
   (or white chocolate)

Repeat until you have all six cakes.

For the buttercream, mix the butter on its own for a few minutes. Then add the icing sugar, vanilla extract and milk and mix until smooth. If using the white food colouring, add it now and mix until it is your desired shade. For the best results, use an electric hand whisk or a stand mixer with paddle attachment. If your buttercream is too stiff, you can add a little more milk to loosen it.

Using a 7cm round cutter, cut out five rounds of cake from each sponge. You can use the leftover cake to make cake truffles – head to page 117 for the recipe.

Place the first colour of cake into the jar, then pipe or dollop some buttercream on top. Don't pipe the buttercream all the way to the edge, as when you add the next layer of cake and push it down, the buttercream will spread out to the edges. Continue until all of the cake is in the jar.

If you want to be able to put the lids on and transport the cake, add a flat swirl of buttercream and some sprinkles.

If you would like to decorate the cake jars as I have, start by making the gold stars. Roll out the modelling paste to 5mm thick. Cut out the stars using fondant or biscuit cutters, the ones I used were 4cm wide and 2.5cm wide. Push cocktail sticks into the stars, then leave to set until the modelling paste has hardened (ideally overnight). Mix about half of the lustre dust with some dipping solution and paint the stars gold, then sprinkle them with edible glitter.

For the chocolate drip, melt the white chocolate and double cream together. I do this in a heatproof bowl in the microwave in blasts of 10-15 seconds, stirring between each one, but you can also do it in a glass bowl over a pan of simmering water. Transfer the white chocolate drip into a piping bag, snip a little bit off the end with some scissors, and pipe varying amounts on the jar, starting just below where the lid screws on, and let it drip down the sides. Chill in the fridge to set fully.

Mix the remaining lustre dust together with the dipping solution, and carefully paint the chocolate drip gold. Melt the white candy melts, again in the microwave in short blasts, stirring between each one. Spread them around the rim of the jar – I used a small paintbrush – and add the sprinkles while the candy is still wet so that they stick. Pipe a big swirl of the buttercream on top of each cake jar. Decorate with the gold stars and more sprinkles. Store in an airtight container in a cool place and eat within 3 days.

Cakes & Cupcakes

Pink Ombre Cake

Ombre means 'to shade' in French and is the art of blending one colour into another. This cake impresses with both its changing pink hues and the beautifully piped rosettes that cover it. Inside are three layers of matching shaded cake with delicious vanilla flavour. This is a showstopping cake that is sure to wow your friends and family, both with its exterior and when you cut into it to reveal the inside.

Prep time: 25 minutes
Bake time: 30–35 minutes
Chill time: 30 minutes
Decorating time: 1 hour
Serves: 16+

500g baking spread, softened
500g caster sugar
9 large eggs
3 tsp vanilla extract
500g self-raising flour
Pink food colouring (I use Colour Mill Hot Pink in the following amounts: 4 drops for layer one, 8 drops for layer two, 11 drops for layer three)

FOR THE BUTTERCREAM

600g unsalted butter, softened
1.2kg icing sugar
3 tsp vanilla extract
3–4 tbsp milk
Pink food colouring (I use Colour Mill Hot Pink in the following amounts: 3 drops for the light pink, 6 drops for the medium pink, 10 drops for the dark pink)

Preheat the oven to 150°C fan/Gas mark 3½ and grease and line three 20cm cake tins at least 5cm deep.

For the cake, mix together the baking spread and sugar, ideally using a stand mixer with the paddle attachment, or an electric hand mixer, for 3–5 minutes until smooth and fluffy. Add the eggs and vanilla extract and whisk well until combined. Gently whisk or fold in the flour. Divide the cake batter into three bowls, using scales for accuracy if you like. Colour each bowl of batter with the pink food colouring. Start with the lightest pink, then increase the food colouring in the next bowl of batter for a medium pink shade, and finally increase it more in the third bowl of batter for a darker pink. Add each colour of cake batter to its own cake tin and spread out into an even layer. Bake for 30–35 minutes, or until risen and a thin skewer inserted into the centre of each cake comes out clean. Leave the cakes to cool completely, either in the tins, or transfer them to wire racks.

For the buttercream, mix the butter on its own for a few minutes. Then add the icing sugar, vanilla extract and milk and mix until smooth. For the best results, use an electric hand whisk or stand mixer with the paddle attachment. If your buttercream is too stiff, you can add a little more milk to loosen it.

Recipe continues overleaf

Cakes & Cupcakes

Level off each cake with a cake leveller or knife. Place the darkest pink cake onto a cake board. To make it easier to decorate, place the cake board onto a decorating turntable with a non-slip mat between them. Spread buttercream over the first layer of cake. Add the medium pink cake layer, more buttercream, then add the third and palest pink cake layer. Cover the whole cake in a thin layer of buttercream (a crumb coat) and smooth it out. Chill the cake in the fridge for 30 minutes to set the buttercream.

Split the remaining buttercream into three bowls and colour with the pink food colouring. You will need half of the buttercream to be light pink (as this colour covers the top of the cake too), a quarter of the buttercream to be medium pink and a quarter of the buttercream to be dark pink. Add each colour of the buttercream to its own piping bag fitted with the same piping nozzle (I used a Wilton 1M). If you only have one piping nozzle, you'll need to cover the other bowls of buttercream, so that they don't dry out, and clean the nozzle in between each use. If you want to practise the rosettes first, you can do so on a piece of baking paper. Once you feel confident, scrape the buttercream back into the piping bag so it does not get wasted.

Measure the height of your cake and divide by three, then using a palette knife, or the blunt side of a butter knife, gently mark indents into the crumb coat of buttercream to indicate each third of the cake. This will help to guide you as you pipe and make each row of rosettes equal in size.

Start by piping the dark pink rosettes all around the bottom third of the cake. When piping, aim to finish piping each rosette where the next rosette will begin, this will create an overlap and ensure there are no big gaps on the cake. Pipe the medium pink buttercream in rosettes all around the middle third of the cake and finally pipe the pale pink buttercream in rosettes all around the top third of the cake and all over the top of the cake. Store any leftovers in an airtight container in a cool place for up to 3 days.

TIP:
You can change the colour of food colouring used in this cake to suit your occasion. You could make a blue, purple or green ombre cake if you like.

CO

OKIES

Strawberry & Cream Cookies

Make it feel like summer in your kitchen any time of year with these gorgeous cookies! They're packed with freeze-dried strawberries for plenty of natural strawberry flavour, without any of the sogginess of fresh ones. The centre is filled with sweetened cream cheese, and they're drizzled with creamy white chocolate.

Prep time: 45 minutes
Chill time: 30 minutes
Bake time: 12–14 minutes
Decorating time: 10 minutes
Makes: 12

125g unsalted butter, softened
125g caster sugar
75g soft light brown sugar
1 large egg
1 tsp vanilla extract
250g plain flour
½ tsp baking powder
¼ tsp salt
¼ tsp bicarbonate of soda
25g freeze-dried strawberries

FOR THE FILLING
75g full-fat cream cheese
20g icing sugar
¼ tsp vanilla extract

FOR DECORATION
50g white chocolate, melted
5g freeze-dried strawberries

For the filling, in a mixing bowl, beat together the cream cheese, icing sugar and vanilla extract with a silicone spatula or a wooden spoon until smooth. Set aside.

Ideally using a stand mixer with the paddle attachment, mix together the butter, caster sugar and light brown sugar until paler in colour and creamy. This will take 3–5 minutes in a stand mixer on a medium speed. Mix in the egg and vanilla extract. Add the flour, baking powder, salt and bicarbonate of soda. Mix until just combined. Add the freeze-dried strawberries and mix briefly until evenly distributed.

Divide the dough into 12 equal portions – I weighed the dough and used 54g per cookie. Roll each portion of dough into a ball using the palms of your hands, then flatten the dough out in your hand. Place 1 teaspoon of the cream cheese filling into the centre of the flattened cookie dough. Fold the cookie dough around the filling and pinch the dough together to seal the cream cheese inside the cookie. Roll it back into a ball and place onto a lined baking tray. Repeat with the remaining cookie dough and filling. Then chill in the freezer for 30 minutes.

Meanwhile, preheat the oven to 180°C fan/Gas Mark 6.

Recipe continues overleaf

Cookies

Place the frozen dough balls onto lined baking trays, leaving at least 5cm between them to allow space to spread. If you don't have enough baking trays, keep some dough in the freezer and bake the cookies in batches for 12–14 minutes. Leave to cool for at least 10 minutes on the baking trays, then transfer to a wire rack to cool completely.

Place the cooled cookies onto some baking paper, then drizzle with the melted white chocolate and sprinkle on the freeze-dried strawberries while the chocolate is still wet so that they stick to it. Leave to set. Store any leftovers in an airtight container in the fridge and eat within 3 days.

Peanut Butter Cookie Cups

Salty peanuts and sweet milk chocolate combine in these cute mini cookie cups. These are made easily in a cupcake tin, the dough is packed with milk chocolate chips and salted peanuts, and the middle is stuffed with creamy peanut butter and a chocolate-covered peanut butter cup. They are absolutely delicious and especially good enjoyed warm.

Prep time: 35 minutes
Bake time: 12–14 minutes
Makes: 12

100g unsalted butter, softened, plus extra for greasing
100g caster sugar
65g soft light brown sugar
1 large egg
1 tsp vanilla extract
215g plain flour
½ tsp baking powder
¼ tsp bicarbonate of soda
100g milk chocolate chips
100g roasted salted peanuts, roughly chopped

FOR THE FILLING
125g smooth peanut butter
12 chocolate-covered peanut butter cups (I use Reese's)

FOR DECORATION
6 roasted salted peanuts, halved

Preheat the oven to 180°C fan/Gas Mark 6 and grease a 12-hole cupcake tin lightly with butter or baking spread.

Ideally using a stand mixer with the paddle attachment, mix together the butter, caster sugar and light brown sugar until fluffy and paler in colour. This will take 3–5 minutes in a stand mixer on a medium speed. Mix in the egg and vanilla extract. Add the flour, baking powder and bicarbonate of soda and mix in until just combined. Briefly mix in the milk chocolate chips and peanuts to evenly distribute them.

Divide the dough into 12 equal portions – I weighed the dough and used 62g per cookie cup. Roll the dough portions into balls using your hands, then place each ball into the hole of the cupcake tin. Use a small cylinder-shaped object, such as the end of a small rolling pin, or the base of a small bottle, to shape the dough into the cupcake tin. You're aiming for it to be pressed up the sides and along the base at a similar thickness, with a dip in the middle that's wide enough to fit the chocolate-covered peanut butter cup.

Bake for 12 minutes, or until golden. The cookie cups will rise in the middle, so use the same tool that you used to shape them to push the middles back down as soon as they come out of the oven.

Recipe continues overleaf

Cookies

Fill the cups with the smooth peanut butter and add a chocolate-covered peanut butter cup to each cookie cup while they are still warm. Top with half a peanut once the peanut butter cups have melted all the way to the middle so that the peanut sticks. Leave until cool enough to handle, then remove from the tin and enjoy warm, or leave to cool completely. Store any leftovers in an airtight container in a cool place for 3 days.

TIP
These cookie cups are amazing served warm with ice cream!

Edible Cookie Dough

Isn't all cookie dough edible, you might ask? While it may be a common occurrence to lick the spoon while baking, it's actually not advised to eat raw baked goods, especially in large quantities. But the good news is that this cookie dough is made with heat-treated flour and no eggs, so you can happily scoff it all up without concern!

Prep time: 30 minutes
Bake time: 8 minutes
Makes: 20

200g plain flour
120g unsalted butter, softened
125g soft light brown sugar
45g caster sugar
2 tsp vanilla extract
30ml whole milk
½ tsp salt
150g chocolate chips (I used a mix of milk chocolate and dark chocolate)

Preheat the oven to 150°C fan/Gas Mark 3.

Spread the flour out evenly onto a lined baking tray. If you let the baking paper hang over the edges of the tray it will help later. Cook the flour for 8 minutes or until it reaches a temperature of 74°C – you can use a probe style thermometer to check this if you like. Leave the flour to cool completely. If it is clumpy, sift it before adding to the cookie dough. Grab both side of the overhanging baking paper and bring them upwards to create a tube, then you can easily tip the flour into a sieve.

Ideally using a stand mixer with the paddle attachment, mix together the butter, light brown sugar and caster sugar until light and fluffy. This will take 3–5 minutes in an electric mixer on a medium speed. Mix in the vanilla extract and milk. Add the baked flour and salt and mix until just combined. Finally, add the chocolate chips and stir gently until evenly distributed throughout the dough. The cookie dough is ready to serve! Roll into balls or dig in with a spoon to enjoy. Store any leftovers in an airtight container either in the fridge for 1 week or the freezer for 3 months.

TIP
Dip the cookie dough balls into melted chocolate to make cookie dough truffles or stir smaller balls of cookie dough into ice cream for homemade cookie dough ice cream.

Brownie Cookies

These are the ultimate fudgy chocolate cookie. As you would expect from their name, they are a brownie batter made into cookies. Speed is essential when getting the brownie batter in the oven in order to achieve the coveted shiny and cracked top. But don't worry, even more relaxed bakers can still enjoy the finished product. Add flaky sea salt for delicious contrast, and tuck into these indulgent treats.

Prep time: 25 minutes
Bake time: 12 minutes
Makes: 12

200g dark chocolate, ideally a high cocoa content (70% cocoa solids)
150g unsalted butter, plus extra for greasing
2 large eggs
100g soft light brown sugar
100g caster sugar
1 tsp vanilla extract
125g plain flour
25g cocoa powder
1 tsp baking powder
¼ tsp salt

FOR DECORATION
1–2 tsp flaky sea salt (optional – but recommended!)

Preheat the oven to 160°C fan/Gas Mark 4 and grease and line your baking trays – I used three large ones.

Melt the chocolate and butter together in a pan on a low heat, stirring occasionally. Remove from the heat and leave to cool for 5 minutes.

In a mixing bowl, using an electric hand whisk, or in the bowl of a stand mixer with the whisk attachment, whisk together the eggs, light brown sugar, caster sugar and vanilla extract for exactly 5 minutes until thick and pale in colour (set a timer for accuracy). Add the melted chocolate mixture, whisking constantly as you pour it in. Gently whisk in the flour, cocoa powder, baking powder and salt. Working quickly, use a 5cm cookie scoop or a large spoon to place spoonfuls of the batter onto the lined baking trays. Leave space between them as they will spread.

Bake for 12 minutes. The sooner you get them in the oven, the more likely you are to achieve the shiny and crackly top. Remove from the oven and sprinkle each cookie with some flaky sea salt. Leave to cool completely on the trays before moving as they will be very delicate. Store in an airtight container in a cool place and eat within 3 days.

Chocolate Hazelnut Cookie Pie

Cookie pies are an epic and eye-catching dessert for sugar-rush lovers! In this cookie pie, the pastry has been replaced with chocolate chip cookie, and the filling is a sweet hazelnut cream spread. This impressive dessert is finished off with a chocolate hazelnut buttercream for the ultimate indulgence.

Prep time: 45 minutes
Bake time: 30 minutes
Chill time: 6 hours
Decorating time: 20 minutes
Serves: 16

220g unsalted butter, softened, plus extra for greasing
200g soft light brown sugar
100g caster sugar
1 large egg
1 tbsp milk
1½ tsp vanilla extract
450g plain flour
1 tsp baking powder
1 tsp salt
¼ tsp bicarbonate of soda
100g milk chocolate chips
100g dark chocolate chips
100g milk chocolate, chopped (I use Kinder chocolate)

FOR THE FILLING
700g white chocolate hazelnut cream spread (I use Black Milk, or try a chocolate hazelnut spread like Nutella)
3 chocolate hazelnut wafer bars (I use Kinder Bueno bars)
80g milk chocolate (I used Kinder chocolate)

Lightly grease the sides of a 20cm springform cake tin (at least 7cm deep) with butter or a baking spread and place a circle of baking paper on the bottom (use a little butter to help it stick to the base).

For the cookie dough, in a mixing bowl, beat together the butter, light brown sugar and caster sugar until creamy, ideally using a stand mixer with the paddle attachment. This will take 3–5 minutes in a stand mixer on a medium speed. Mix in the egg, milk and vanilla extract until well combined. Add the flour, baking powder, salt and bicarbonate of soda and mix in. If using a stand mixer, you may need to scrape the bowl down to make sure all of the flour is mixed in. Next, add all the chocolate chips and the chopped chocolate and mix briefly to evenly distribute them throughout the dough. Weigh the dough and spilt it into three pieces (my cookie dough weighed 1,343g in total, so it was 447g per piece).

Press the first piece into the base of the tin and flatten it out until it is evenly spread across the base. You can use your fingers or the back of a spoon to do this. Use the second piece to cover the sides of the tin. Take chunks of it and make a rough sausage shape, then flatten them out around the sides, making sure there are no gaps. Wrap the third piece in clingfilm and set aside on a work surface.

Recipe continues overleaf

FOR DECORATION

(optional)

100g unsalted butter, softened

100g chocolate hazelnut spread (I use Nutella)

200g icing sugar

1–2 tbsp milk

1 chocolate hazelnut wafer bar (I use Kinder Bueno bars)

40g milk chocolate (I use Kinder chocolate)

Warm up the white chocolate hazelnut cream spread in a heatproof bowl in the microwave for 20–30 seconds to loosen it to a pourable consistency. Pour about half of it into the tin lined with the cookie dough. Press the chocolate hazelnut wafer bars and milk chocolate into the spread – you will need to break them up to get them all to fit. Then pour over the remaining spread. Chill in the freezer for 1 hour to firm up.

Flatten the final piece of cookie dough into a disc and cover the top of the pie with it, making sure to seal the edges so the spread is completely enclosed. Return to the freezer for 1 hour. When the hour is almost up, preheat the oven to 180°C fan/Gas Mark 6.

Place the pie onto a baking tray and bake for 30 minutes. I like to put a baking tray beneath it in case a few drops of butter escape from the tin. Leave to cool completely in the tin, then transfer to the fridge for 4–5 hours or ideally overnight.

Remove the pie from the tin. If you would like to decorate it with the buttercream, mix the butter and chocolate hazelnut spread together, ideally using a stand mixer with the paddle attachment or an electric hand mixer, until creamy. Add the icing sugar and milk and mix until smooth. Transfer the buttercream into a piping bag fitted with the nozzle of your choice, and pipe it around the edge of the cookie pie. Decorate with the chocolate hazelnut wafer bar and chunks of milk chocolate. To serve, slice into pieces using a sharp knife. Store any leftovers in an airtight container in a cool place and eat within 3–4 days.

Sandwich Cookies

Why have one chocolate chip cookie, when you can have two? Plus, a luxuriously light whipped ganache in the middle, and lots of pretty sprinkles. These sandwich cookies are the yummiest sandwich around. Although they can be cut in half and shared, you'll find it tricky to do once you've taken a bite!

Prep time: 40 minutes
Chill time: 30 minutes
Bake time: 12–14 minutes
Decorating time: 20 minutes
Makes: 8

125g unsalted butter, softened
125g caster sugar
75g soft light brown sugar
1 large egg
1 tsp vanilla extract
250g plain flour
½ tsp baking powder
¼ tsp bicarbonate of soda
¼ tsp salt
200g milk chocolate chips

FOR THE FILLING
200ml double cream
200g dark chocolate

FOR DECORATION
15g sprinkles

For the chocolate ganache filling, heat the cream in a pan on a low heat until it starts to steam. Remove from the heat, add the chocolate and leave it for 5 minutes. Stir until the chocolate is fully melted into the double cream. Set aside to cool completely.

Ideally using a stand mixer with the paddle attachment, mix together the butter, caster sugar and light brown sugar until fluffy and pale in colour. This will take 3–5 minutes in a stand mixer on a medium speed. Mix in the egg and vanilla extract. Add the flour, baking powder, bicarbonate of soda and salt and mix in until just combined. Briefly mix in the chocolate chips to evenly distribute them. Divide the dough into 16 equal portions – I weighed the dough and used 51g per cookie. Roll the dough portions into balls using your hands, then place them on either a lined baking tray, or into an airtight container lined with baking paper. Chill in the fridge for 30 minutes.

Meanwhile, preheat the oven to 180°C fan/Gas Mark 6.

Place the dough balls onto lined baking trays, leaving at least 5cm between them to allow room to spread. If you don't have enough baking trays, keep the dough in the fridge and bake the cookies in batches. Bake for 12–14 minutes, or until lightly golden and they don't look raw in the centre. Leave to cool for at least 10 minutes on the baking trays, then transfer to a wire rack to cool completely.

Recipe continues overleaf

Cookies

Put the cooled ganache filling in a mixing bowl and whisk, ideally using a stand mixer with the whisk attachment, or an electric hand mixer, for 2 minutes until lighter in colour. Spread or pipe the ganache onto half of the cookies, then sandwich them together with the remaining cookies.

Spread the sprinkles out on a plate and gently dip the sides of the cookies into them, turning as you go so the sprinkles cover the ganache all the way around. Store any leftovers in an airtight container and eat within 3 days.

Speculoos Stuffed Chocolate Cookies

These chocolate cookies have a dreamy speculoos centre and are packed with white chocolate chips too. Adding a filling to cookies, especially something everyone loves like speculoos, really takes your cookie baking to the next level.

Prep time: 25 minutes
Chill time: 30 minutes
Bake time: 12–14 minutes
Makes: 12

125g unsalted butter, softened
75g caster sugar
125g soft light brown sugar
1 large egg
1 tsp vanilla extract
215g plain flour
35g cocoa powder
½ tsp baking powder
¼ tsp bicarbonate of soda
¼ tsp salt
200g white chocolate chips

FOR THE FILLING
120g smooth speculoos spread (I use Biscoff)

FOR DECORATION
45g smooth speculoos spread (I use Biscoff)

Ideally using a stand mixer with the paddle attachment, mix together the butter, caster sugar and light brown sugar until fluffy and pale in colour. This will take 3–5 minutes in a stand mixer on a medium speed. Mix in the egg and vanilla extract. Add the flour, cocoa powder, baking powder, bicarbonate of soda and salt and mix in until just combined. Briefly mix in the chocolate chips to evenly distribute them.

Divide the dough into 12 equal portions – I weighed it and used 68g per cookie. Roll the dough portions into balls using your hands, then flatten them out into discs. Place 1 teaspoon (about 10g) of speculoos spread in the centre of each cookie. Wrap the dough around the speculoos spread, enclosing it inside, and roll the dough back into a ball using your hands. Place the filled cookie balls onto either a lined baking tray, or into a plastic container lined with baking paper. Chill in the freezer for 30 minutes.

Meanwhile, preheat the oven to 180°C fan/Gas Mark 6.

Place the dough balls onto lined baking trays, leaving at least 5cm between them to allow space to spread. If you don't have enough baking trays, keep the dough in the freezer and bake the cookies in batches. Bake for 12–14 minutes, or until they don't look raw in the centre. Leave to cool for at least 10 minutes on the baking trays, then transfer to a wire rack.

To decorate, warm the speculoos spread in a heatproof bowl in the microwave for 10–15 seconds. You can pipe it over the cookies or drizzle it over with a spoon. Serve warm for the ultimate gooey centre! Store any leftovers in an airtight container and eat within 3 days.

Sprinkle Cookies

Sprinkles make everything more fun and these easy cookies are no exception. They are colourful inside and out, with rainbow sprinkles and white chocolate chips both in the batter and as decoration. They're great for baking with kids and will brighten up your day as well as any event you take them to.

Prep time: 30 minutes
Chill time: 30 minutes
Bake time: 12–14 minutes
Decorating time: 15 minutes
Makes: 14

125g unsalted butter, softened
125g caster sugar
75g soft light brown sugar
1 large egg
1 tsp vanilla extract
250g plain flour
½ tsp baking powder
¼ tsp bicarbonate of soda
¼ tsp salt
175g white chocolate chips
60g rainbow sprinkles

FOR DECORATION
50g white chocolate, melted
15g rainbow sprinkles

Ideally using a stand mixer with the paddle attachment, mix together the butter, caster sugar and light brown sugar until fluffy and pale in colour. This will take 3–5 minutes in a stand mixer on a medium speed. Mix in the egg and vanilla extract. Add the flour, baking powder, bicarbonate of soda and salt and mix in until combined. Then briefly mix in the chocolate chips and sprinkles, just to evenly distribute them. Divide the dough into 14 equal portions – I weighed the dough and used 65g per cookie. Roll the dough portions into balls using your hands, place them on either a lined baking tray, or into a plastic container lined with baking paper. Chill in the fridge for 30 minutes.

Meanwhile, preheat the oven to 180°C fan/Gas Mark 6.

Place the dough balls onto lined baking trays, leaving at least 5cm between them to allow room to spread. If you don't have enough baking trays, keep the dough in the fridge and bake the cookies in batches. Bake for 12–14 minutes, or until lightly golden and they don't look raw in the centre. Leave to cool for at least 10 minutes on the baking trays, then transfer to a wire rack to cool completely.

To decorate, you can pipe on the melted chocolate or drizzle it over with a spoon. Add the sprinkles while the chocolate is still wet, so that they stick to it. Store any leftovers in an airtight container and eat within 3 days.

Cookie Dippers

Have you ever struggled to dip a round cookie into your glass of milk or cup of tea? Me too! Well, these cookie dippers are the answer. Chocolate chip cookie dough is baked in a square tin and cut into long rectangles, so you can grab one end and dip the other in your chosen beverage. Or, for an upgrade on tea and milk, I recommend dipping them in some warm salted caramel sauce for an absolutely heavenly experience.

Prep time: 25 minutes
Bake time: 25 minutes
Makes: 16

125g unsalted butter, softened, plus extra for greasing
100g caster sugar
100g soft light brown sugar
1 large egg
1 tsp vanilla extract
250g plain flour
½ tsp baking powder
¼ tsp bicarbonate of soda
¼ tsp salt
200g milk chocolate chips

TO SERVE
200g ready-made salted caramel sauce

Preheat the oven to 160°C fan/Gas Mark 4 and line a 23cm square tin with baking paper, greasing the tin with a little butter first to help the paper stick to it.

Ideally using a stand mixer with the paddle attachment, mix together the butter, caster sugar and light brown sugar until fluffy and pale in colour. This will take 3–5 minutes in a stand mixer on a medium speed. Mix in the egg and vanilla extract. Add the flour, baking powder, bicarbonate of soda and salt and mix in until just combined. Briefly mix in 175g of the chocolate chips to evenly distribute them. Press the cookie dough into the tin and smooth out into an even layer. Sprinkle over the remaining 25g chocolate chips. Bake for 25 minutes, or until lightly golden all over. Leave to cool completely in the tin.

Remove from the tin and slice in half, then slice each half into eight fingers. Serve with the caramel sauce for dipping. Depending on the texture, you can warm the sauce in the microwave first. Store any leftover cookie dippers in an airtight container and eat within 3 days. Check the container of the sauce you have used for storage details.

TIP
The cookie dippers are also delicious dipped in cold milk, tea, coffee, hot chocolate and melted chocolate hazelnut or speculoos spread.

NO-
T

BAKE REATS

No-Boil Chocolate Orange Fudge

This easy recipe will revolutionise the way you make fudge. There's no boiling involved, making it a much simpler process. Milk and dark chocolate are melted together with condensed milk, then combined with icing sugar and packed with chocolate orange pieces. A few hours later and it sets into a perfect fudgy texture that melts in the mouth. This fudge makes a great edible gift option for your friends and family – if you can bear to let it leave your house!

Prep time: 25 minutes
Chill time: 3–4 hours
Makes: 36

Unsalted butter, for greasing
397g tin condensed milk
100g dark chocolate
300g milk chocolate
130g icing sugar, sifted
1 chocolate orange ball (I use Terry's Chocolate Orange)

FOR DECORATION (OPTIONAL)
50g white chocolate
Orange food colouring
Orange sprinkles

Line a 20cm square tin with baking paper, greasing it with a little butter to help the paper stick to it.

Melt the condensed milk, dark chocolate and milk chocolate together in a pan on a low heat, stirring together as it melts. Once it's fully melted and combined, take the pan off the heat and stir in the icing sugar. Pour half of the mixture into the tin, smooth it down and press some of the chocolate orange pieces into it. Pour the remaining fudge mixture over the top, and smooth down.

If you want to decorate the fudge, melt the white chocolate in a heatproof bowl in the microwave (blast for 30 seconds, stir, then blast in 10 second intervals, stirring between each one) or over a pan of simmering water. Colour it bright orange with the food colouring. Add blobs of the melted chocolate to the top of the fudge and use a cocktail stick to swirl it around. Add the remaining chocolate orange pieces on top, breaking them in half if needed and pressing them in. Add some sprinkles if you like, then chill in the fridge for at least 3–4 hours, or overnight, to set. To serve, remove from the tin and slice into pieces using a sharp knife. Store in the fridge for 2–3 weeks.

No-Bake Vanilla Cheesecake

No-bake cheesecakes are my favourite no-bake treats – I've made countless variations and flavours over the years. This is my classic vanilla cheesecake recipe, it's super creamy, lightly sweet and has an incredible mousse-like texture. It really is totally different from baked cheesecake. This is the perfect recipe to introduce you to the world of no-bake cheesecakes, and you can get as creative as you like with the decoration too!

Prep time: 40 minutes
Chill time: 4+ hours
Serves: 16

300g digestive biscuits, crushed
135g unsalted butter or baking spread, melted

FOR THE FILLING
750g full-fat cream cheese
125g icing sugar
2 tsp vanilla extract
300ml double cream

FOR DECORATION (OPTIONAL)
Melted chocolate
Caramel sauce
150ml double cream
½ tbsp icing sugar
½ tsp vanilla extract
Chocolate stars
Sprinkles

To make the biscuit base, use a food processor to blitz the digestive biscuits into crumbs, or put them in a bowl or a freezer bag and bash them gently with a rolling pin. Add the melted butter to the biscuit crumbs and mix them together. Press the mixture into the bottom of a 23cm round springform tin. Chill in the fridge for 30 minutes while you make the filling.

For the cheesecake filling, use a stand mixer with the whisk attachment or an electric hand whisk to mix together the cream cheese, icing sugar and vanilla extract until smooth with no lumps. Add the cream and whisk until it is very thick and holds its shape. When you scoop it up with a spoon it should not slide off easily. Smooth the mixture evenly on top of the biscuit base, then chill in the fridge for at least 4 hours, or overnight, to set.

Remove from the tin and put on your serving plate. Smooth the sides with a butter knife to create a neater finish. To decorate, drizzle over the melted chocolate and caramel sauce. Whip the cream with the icing sugar and vanilla extract, and pipe it all around the top edge of the cheesecake. Decorate with the chocolate stars and sprinkles. Serve immediately. Store any leftovers in the fridge and eat within 2–3 days.

No-Bake Treats

65

Jam Sandwich Biscuit No-Churn Ice Cream

Prep time: 40 minutes
Chill time: 4+ hours
Serves: 16

397g tin condensed milk
1 tsp vanilla extract
600ml double cream
50g white chocolate chips
6 jam sandwich biscuits,
    chopped (I use Jammie
    Dodgers)
175g raspberry jam

FOR DECORATION
25g raspberry jam
3 jam sandwich biscuits,
    halved (I use Jammie
    Dodgers)
7 mini jam sandwich
    biscuits (I use Jammie
    Dodgers)
2 tsp freeze-dried
    raspberries (optional)

Jam sandwich biscuits take me back to childhood and they are the stars of the show in this creamy dessert. Chunks of jam sandwich biscuits have been swirled through vanilla ice cream, along with white chocolate chips and raspberry jam. You don't need an ice-cream maker for this recipe, just an electric mixer or a very strong arm!

In a mixing bowl, mix the condensed milk and vanilla extract together using a hand whisk or spatula. In another bowl, use an electric hand mixer to whip the cream until soft peaks form, or you can do this in a stand mixer with the whisk attachment. Gently fold the cream into the condensed milk mixture using a spoon or spatula. Fold in the white chocolate chips and chopped jam sandwich biscuits. Very gently swirl in the jam, making sure you don't overmix it as you want to leave swirls of jam throughout the ice cream.

Put the ice cream into a 2.5-litre tub, or split between smaller tubs, then decorate the top with the jam, jam sandwich biscuits and freeze-dried raspberries if you have some. Chill in the freezer for at least 4 hours, or overnight. Store in the freezer for up to 3 months.

Coffee Mug Cake

Sometimes you just need to satisfy a cake craving ASAP, and that's where mug cakes come to the rescue! There's minimal washing up and virtually no effort involved, but with a delicious result. This Coffee Mug Cake not only levels up the cake-to-mouth waiting time, but it also makes getting your caffeine fix a lot tastier. Add ice cream or whipped cream for extra indulgence.

Prep time: 10 minutes
Cook time: 1 hour
Serves: 1

70g self-raising flour
3 tsp instant coffee
30g soft light brown sugar
Pinch of salt
80ml milk
25ml vegetable oil
½ tsp vanilla extract

TO SERVE
2 scoops of vanilla
    ice cream
Cocoa powder,
    for dusting

You will need one 350ml mug that is microwave safe.

Add the flour, coffee, sugar and salt to the mug and stir to combine. Add the milk, vegetable oil and vanilla extract and, ideally using a fork, mix until all the ingredients are fully combined. It's worth using a spoon to check there's no unmixed flour at the very bottom of the mug.

Put the mug onto a microwave-safe plate and microwave in a 900W microwave for 2½ minutes. Add the scoops of ice cream and a dusting of cocoa powder, then tuck in!

Easter Egg Cheesecake

This cheesecake is a simple dessert for Easter time! It's a chocolate egg shell filled with a creamy no-bake cheesecake, layered over a biscuit base. If you're looking for an easy seasonal dessert that everyone will love, then you have found it. You can make this in advance and customise it with your favourite Easter treats. Children will love to get involved in making these yummy cheesecake-filled Easter eggs too.

Prep time: 30 minutes
Chill time: 2 hours
Serves: 4

1 large Easter egg (approx. 150g)
60g digestive biscuits
25g unsalted butter or baking spread, melted

FOR THE FILLING
235g full-fat cream cheese
40g icing sugar
1 tsp vanilla extract
95ml double cream

FOR DECORATION (OPTIONAL)
Caramel sauce
Milk chocolate, melted
Mini chocolate eggs
Mini fondant-filled chocolate eggs

To cut the Easter egg in half, warm a large sharp knife under a hot water tap. Carefully dry it, then very gently press it around the egg where the seam is. Keep slowly and gently working your way around the egg, re-warming the knife if needed, until the two halves separate.

To make the biscuit base, use a food processor to blitz the digestive biscuits into crumbs, or put them in a bowl or a freezer bag and bash them gently with a rolling pin. Add the melted butter to the biscuit crumbs and mix them together. Divide the biscuit base evenly between the Easter egg halves, using the back of a small spoon to press it down gently until it is compact and even. Chill in the fridge while you make the filling.

To make the cheesecake filling, mix the cream cheese, icing sugar and vanilla extract in a mixing bowl with an electric hand mixer until smooth. Add the cream and mix until thick and the filling holds its shape. Divide the filling between the Easter egg halves and use a small palette knife, or the back of a small spoon, to gently press the mixture into them and smooth the top. Chill in the fridge for 2 hours to set.

Decorate with caramel sauce, melted chocolate, mini chocolate eggs and mini fondant-filled chocolate eggs – or any Easter treats you prefer. Serve immediately, or store in the fridge for 3–4 days.

Neapolitan Cheesecake Jars

These cheesecake jars are inspired by Neapolitan ice cream, which brings back so many childhood memories for me. I would always eat the vanilla and chocolate layers, while my brother would happily take care of the strawberry. Nowadays I love them all and even more so in cheesecake form. Serving them in jars is such a cute effect and shows off their pretty layers perfectly. They're great for dinner parties too as you can make them ahead of time.

Prep time: 45 minutes
Chill time: 1 hour
Makes: 4

130g digestive biscuits, crushed
70g unsalted butter or baking spread, melted

FOR THE CHEESECAKE
475g full-fat cream cheese
75g icing sugar
475ml double cream
3 drops of pink food colouring
4 drops of strawberry flavouring (I use LorAnn, you may need more or less flavouring depending on the kind you use)
1½ tsp vanilla extract
2 tbsp cocoa powder

FOR DECORATION
150ml double cream
½ tbsp icing sugar
½ tsp vanilla extract
4 strawberries

For the biscuit base, use a food processor to blitz the digestive biscuits into crumbs, or put them in a bowl or a freezer bag and bash them gently with a rolling pin. Add the melted butter to the biscuit crumbs and mix them together. Divide the biscuit mixture between your jars – I used 50g per jar. Press them down into the bottom of the jar using the base of a small rolling pin or the back of a teaspoon. Chill in the fridge while you make the cheesecake.

To make the cheesecake, use an electric hand mixer to mix the cream cheese and icing sugar together until smooth. Add the double cream and whisk until the mixture thickens and holds its shape. Divide the cheesecake mixture equally between three bowls. In the first bowl, mix in the pink food colouring and strawberry flavouring. In the second bowl, mix in the vanilla extract. In the third bowl, mix in the cocoa powder.

Split the strawberry cheesecake between your serving jars – I used around 83g of each cheesecake mixture per jar. You can spoon or pipe each cheesecake mixture into the jars. Once you've added the vanilla layer, smooth it out as best you can before adding the next chocolate layer of cheesecake.

Recipe continues overleaf

For decoration, use an electric hand mixer, a stand mixer with the whisk attachment, or a strong arm to whisk the cream, icing sugar and vanilla extract until it is thick and holds its shape. Pipe or dollop it on top of each cheesecake. Decorate with a fresh strawberry. Chill for 1–2 hours, then serve. Any leftovers can be kept in the fridge for up to 2 days.

TIP

You could also decorate the cheesecake jars with chocolate sauce or other fresh fruits.

No-Bake Treats

Mint Chocolate Rocky Road

Rocky road is one of the easiest and most delicious treats around. The only hard part? Waiting for it to set! This Mint Chocolate Rocky Road is packed with biscuits, marshmallows and an assortment of mint chocolate favourites. Trust me, it will be more than worth the wait. Rocky road is great for sharing too and lasts for a few weeks in the fridge, so it's great for making ahead of time.

Prep time: 25 minutes
Chill time: 3–4 hours
Serves: 16

100g digestive biscuits, broken into pieces
75g mini marshmallows (gelatine-free if serving to vegetarians)
90g bubbly mint chocolate (I use Aero Peppermint)
75g mint chocolate balls (I use Aero Bubbles)
50g mint chocolate sticks (I use Matchmakers)
55g mint chocolate fondant squares (I use After Eight)
200g unsalted butter, plus extra for greasing
200g milk chocolate
300g dark chocolate
150g golden syrup

FOR DECORATION

120g mint chocolate balls (I use Aero Bubbles)
55g mint chocolate fondant squares (I use After Eight)
50g mint chocolate sticks (I use Matchmakers)
20g white chocolate
2–3 drops green food colouring

Line a 20cm square tin with baking paper. I grease the tin first with a little butter to help the paper stick to it.

In a mixing bowl, add the digestive biscuits, the mini marshmallows, the bubbly mint chocolate, the mint chocolate balls, the mint chocolate sticks and the mint chocolate fondant squares, chopping or breaking up any big chocolate pieces.

Put the butter, milk chocolate, dark chocolate and golden syrup in a pan and melt on a low heat, stirring together. Once fully melted and combined, take the pan off the heat and leave to cool for 5 minutes.

Pour about three-quarters of the chocolate mixture into the bowl of digestive biscuits and mint chocolates and stir to fully coat with the chocolate mixture. Pour into the lined tin, spread out into an even layer, then pour over the remaining chocolate mixture to fill in any gaps. Give the tin a gentle shake and tap it on a work surface a couple of times to remove any air bubbles.

Decorate the top with more of the mint chocolates, chopping or breaking them up as needed. Chill in the fridge for at least 3–4 hours, or overnight, to set.

Recipe continues overleaf

To decorate, melt the white chocolate in a heatproof bowl in the microwave (blast for 30 seconds, stir, then blast in 10-second intervals, stirring between each one) or over a pan of simmering water. Then mix in the green food colouring.

Drizzle the green chocolate all over the rocky road, using a piping bag or a spoon. Once the green chocolate has set, remove the rocky road from the tin and slice into pieces using a sharp knife. Store any leftovers in the fridge for up to 3 weeks.

TRAY

BAKES

Cookies & Cream Blondies

Blondies are the white chocolate sisters of brownies; they are soft and gooey with a smooth vanilla flavour. This cookies and cream version is packed with cookies and cream biscuits and white chocolate chips. They're fudgy, crunchy and very addictive! The best thing about them is how simple they are to make, so bakers of any level can get involved in a blondie baking session.

Prep time: 25 minutes
Bake time: 30–35 minutes
Chill time: 2 hours
Makes: 16

250g unsalted butter, plus extra for greasing
300g golden caster sugar (or regular caster sugar)
250g white chocolate, broken into chunks
3 large eggs
1 tsp vanilla extract
250g plain flour
150g white chocolate chips
200g cookies and cream biscuits, broken into pieces (I use Oreo)

FOR DECORATION
65g cookies and cream biscuits, broken into pieces (I use Oreo)

Preheat the oven to 160°C fan/Gas Mark 4 and grease and line a 23cm square tin.

Melt the butter and sugar in a pan on a low heat, stirring together as it melts. Remove from the heat, add the white chocolate and leave it for a few minutes. Then stir together to melt the chocolate into the mixture. Leave to cool for 5 minutes. Don't worry if it looks a little lumpy. You can transfer the mixture to a mixing bowl at this point, or leave it in the pan and continue. Whisk in the eggs and vanilla extract using a hand whisk. Whisk in the flour until fully combined. Gently fold in the white chocolate chips and broken cookies and cream biscuits. Pour the mixture into the tin, spread it out evenly, then sprinkle the cookie sandwich biscuits for decoration on top.

Bake for 30–35 minutes, or until lightly golden all over. Leave to cool fully in the tin, then chill in the fridge for 2 hours. To serve, slice into squares using a sharp knife. Store in an airtight container in a cool place and eat within 3 days.

TIP
You can also make the blondies in a traybake-style tin (30 x 23cm) and bake for 25–30 minutes.

Chocolate Hazelnut Loaded Flapjacks

I decided to level up my flapjacks and load them with tasty toppings for extra indulgence and an impressive finish. These flapjacks are covered in white chocolate that's swirled with chocolate hazelnut spread, then decorated with chocolate hazelnut wafer bars and milk chocolate bars. You'll be very popular when you come out of the kitchen with these treats!

Prep time: 25 minutes
Bake time: 20–25 minutes
Decorating time: 20 minutes
Setting time: 1–2 hours
Makes: 9

350g porridge oats
Pinch of salt
200g unsalted butter, plus extra for greasing
175g soft light brown sugar
100g golden syrup

FOR DECORATION
300g white chocolate
75g chocolate hazelnut spread (I use Nutella)
2½ chocolate hazelnut wafer bars (I use Kinder Bueno)
3½ milk chocolate bars (I use Kinder chocolate)

Preheat the oven to 160°C fan/Gas Mark 4 and grease and line a 20cm square baking tin.

In a large mixing bowl, add the porridge oats and salt and stir together. Melt the butter, sugar and golden syrup in a pan on a low heat, stirring occasionally. Pour the melted butter mixture into the oats and stir until the oats are fully coated. Pour the mixture into the tin and press down into an even layer. Bake for 20–25 minutes until golden and bubbling. The flapjacks won't look set but don't worry they will firm up as they cool. Leave to cool completely in the tin.

To decorate, melt the white chocolate in a heatproof bowl in the microwave (blast for 30 seconds, stir, then blast in 10-second intervals, stirring between each one) or over a pan of simmering water. Spread the melted chocolate over the flapjacks and smooth out. Warm the chocolate hazelnut spread briefly in a heatproof bowl in the microwave (20–30 seconds), then add spoonfuls of it all over the white chocolate. Use a butter knife to swirl the chocolate hazelnut spread into the white chocolate. Decorate with the chunks of chocolate hazelnut wafer bars and milk chocolate bars. Leave the white chocolate to set for 1–2 hours. Cut into squares using a sharp knife and serve. Store leftovers in an airtight container in a cool place for up to 1 week.

TIP
You can also use a 23cm square tin for this recipe, the flapjacks will just be a little thinner. You may also need a few more toppings to decorate the flapjacks if using a bigger tin.

Raspberry & White Chocolate Millionaire's Shortbread

This delicious twist on millionaire's shortbread features a buttery shortbread base that's packed with white chocolate chips and freeze-dried raspberries. In the middle is the classic gooey caramel, and on top is more white chocolate and plenty of freeze-dried raspberries. This version of millionaire's shortbread is so summery and pretty, you may even like it more than the original!

Prep time: 45 minutes
Bake time: 25 minutes
Setting time: 3 hours
Makes: 16

80g caster sugar
1 tsp vanilla extract
200g unsalted butter, softened
225g plain flour
10g freeze-dried raspberries
50g white chocolate chips

FOR THE CARAMEL
170g unsalted butter
80g golden syrup
75g granulated sugar
397g tin condensed milk

FOR DECORATION
225g white chocolate
10g freeze-dried raspberries

Preheat the oven to 160°C fan/Gas Mark 4 and line a 20cm square tin with baking paper, greasing the tin with a little butter first to help the paper stick to it.

To make the shortbread biscuit base, mix the sugar, vanilla extract and butter together, ideally using a stand mixer with the paddle attachment, for 3 minutes. Add the flour and mix in until a dough forms. Briefly mix in the freeze-dried raspberries and chocolate chips until evenly distributed. Press the shortbread base into the tin with your fingers until compact and even. Bake for 25 minutes until lightly golden. Leave to cool fully in the tin.

To make the caramel, put all the ingredients in a pan on a low heat and stir until everything is melted together. Bring to the boil, stirring continuously, and boil for 5–7 minutes until thick and golden. This instruction is for gas hobs; for induction hobs, I find that simmering for 10–12 minutes works best. Ultimately you are aiming for a golden colour and for the mixture to have thickened noticeably. Take the mixture off the heat, then pour the caramel over the top of the shortbread base, smooth it out with a palette knife or the back of a spoon if needed. Chill in the fridge for at least 2 hours to set, or overnight if you prefer. Bring it back to room temperature before you add the chocolate layer.

Recipe continues overleaf

To decorate, melt the chocolate in a heatproof bowl in the microwave (blast for 30 seconds, stir, then blast in 10-second intervals, stirring between each one) or over a pan of simmering water. Pour the chocolate over the caramel and smooth it out, tap the tin onto a work surface a few times to remove any air bubbles and to create an even surface. Sprinkle over the freeze-dried raspberries. Leave at room temperature for the chocolate to set fully.

It is best to slice this shortbread at room temperature to avoid cracking the chocolate top. Remove the millionaire's shortbread from the tin and peel off the baking paper. Slice carefully using a large sharp knife – it helps if the length of the knife is longer than the shortbread. Use a gentle sawing motion to cut through the chocolate layer, then push the knife down to slice through the remaining layers. Store any leftovers in an airtight container in a cool place and eat within 1 week.

Black Forest Brownies

Cherries and chocolate combine in this gooey traybake treat. Rich and moist chocolate brownies are stuffed with cherry chunks and dark chocolate chips for the ultimate indulgence. Cherry jam is swirled into the batter before baking for a gorgeous marbled effect. Of course, you can't have black forest without a generous dollop of whipped cream, which I highly recommend serving alongside these brownies. And for the grown-ups, why not add a dram of kirsch too.

Prep time: 30 minutes
Bake time: 30 minutes
Chill time: 2 hours
Makes: 12

350g dark chocolate
250g unsalted butter, plus extra for greasing
250g soft dark brown sugar
3 large eggs
120g plain flour
200g tinned cherries, drained and chopped
125g dark chocolate chips
85g cherry jam
1 tbsp kirsch (optional)

TO SERVE
Whipped cream
Cherries (fresh or glacé)
Dark chocolate shavings

Preheat the oven to 160°C fan/Gas Mark 4 and grease and line a 23cm square baking tin.

Melt the dark chocolate and butter together in a pan on a low heat, stirring occasionally. Set aside to cool for 5 minutes.

In a mixing bowl, using an electric hand whisk, or the whisk attachment of a stand mixer, whisk together the sugar and the eggs for 5 minutes (set a timer for accuracy). Slowly pour in the melted chocolate mixture, constantly whisking on a slow speed. Gently mix in the flour. Fold in the cherries and chocolate chips. Pour the brownie batter into the tin. If using, mix the kirsch into the cherry jam. Add spoonfuls of jam on top of the brownie batter, then use a butter knife to gently swirl the jam into the batter.

Bake for 30 minutes, or until a toothpick inserted into the centre comes out with several moist crumbs on but is not overly wet. Leave it to cool completely, then chill in the fridge for at least 2 hours. Remove from the tin and cut into squares. Serve with whipped cream, either fresh or glacé cherries depending on the season and chocolate shavings. Store in an airtight container in a cool place and eat within 3 days.

TIP

I find tinned cherries really easy to use as they are available all year round, usually already pitted and are always lovely and juicy. You can, however, use fresh cherries for the brownies if you prefer, just make sure to remove the stones first.

Iced Biscuit Cereal Treats

There's something about cereal treats that I can never resist. I find this crunchy rice cereal, stuck together with a gooey marshmallow and butter mixture absolutely moreish. I've added a cute retro twist to this version with a white chocolate topping and some iced ring biscuits. They are quick and easy to make ahead without having to turn the oven on, and they're brilliant party treats. Plus, they look super cute!

Prep time: 30 minutes
Setting time: 1 hour
Makes: 16

200g rice cereal (I use Rice Krispies)
⅛ tsp salt
115g unsalted butter
275g white marshmallows (gelatine-free if serving to vegetarians)
1 tsp vanilla extract
75g mini pink and white marshmallows (gelatine-free if serving to vegetarians)

FOR DECORATION
300g white chocolate, melted
8 iced ring biscuits (I use Party Rings)
16 mini iced ring biscuits (I use Mini Party Rings)
Sprinkles

Grease and line a 23cm square baking tin.

Pour the rice cereal into a large mixing bowl, add the salt and stir together.

Put the butter, white marshmallows and vanilla extract in a pan on a low heat and stir together until the butter and marshmallows are melted. Pour the melted marshmallow mixture into the rice cereal and stir through to fully coat the cereal. Add the mini marshmallows and stir them through until evenly distributed. Press the mixture gently into the tin in an even layer.

To decorate, melt the chocolate in a heatproof bowl in the microwave (blast for 30 seconds, stir, then blast in 10-second intervals, stirring between each one) or over a pan of simmering water. Spread the melted white chocolate over the rice cereal treats. Add the iced ring biscuits and sprinkles to decorate. Leave to set for 1 hour. Cut into squares using a sharp knife and serve. Store any leftovers in an airtight container in a cool place for up to 1 week.

School Dinner Cake

If you were part of the school dinner club, you will recognise this retro dessert. A generous hunk of fluffy vanilla cake is topped with simple white icing and colourful sprinkles. It's served in a puddle of warm custard for ultimate comfort food vibes. This is one of the simplest cakes to make, but gives such an epic and tasty result. It is a dessert everyone will love!

Prep Time: 25 minutes
Bake time: 30–35 minutes
Decorating time: 15 minutes
Serves: 12

350g baking spread, softened, plus extra for greasing
350g caster sugar
6 large eggs
2 tsp vanilla extract
350g self-raising flour
115ml semi-skimmed milk
Store-bought custard, to serve

FOR DECORATION
300g icing sugar
1½ tsp vanilla extract
2–3 tbsp milk
1–2 tbsp sprinkles

TO SERVE:
(optional) 150g store-bought custard per person.

Preheat the oven to 150°C fan/Gas Mark 3½ and grease and line a 30 x 23cm traybake tin.

Mix together the baking spread and sugar, ideally using an electric hand whisk or a stand mixer with the paddle attachment, for 3 minutes until smooth and fluffy. Add the eggs and vanilla extract and mix them in well. Gently whisk or fold in the flour and milk. Pour the mixture into the tin and smooth it out into an even layer. Bake for 35 minutes, or until a thin skewer inserted into the centre comes out clean. Transfer to a wire rack to cool completely – you can either leave the sponge in the tin or remove it and place it directly onto the rack.

To make the icing, mix the icing sugar, vanilla extract and milk together. Add the milk slowly as you may not need it all, you are aiming for a thick but spreadable consistency. Spread the icing over the sponge and add the sprinkles while it is still wet so they will stick to it. Cut the sponge into squares and serve alone, or ideally with warmed custard. Store any leftovers in an airtight container in a cool place for up to 3 days.

Brookies

If you're struggling to decide whether you're craving a brownie or a cookie, then why not have both?! This traybake treat is known by several names – ultimate brownie, brookies, cookie dough brownies – whatever you call them, they're an epic bake that you have to try. They have a chocolate chip cookie base layer and a brownie top, plus bonus cookies and cream biscuits stuffed in the middle. They're a gooey, chewy, sweet bite of heaven.

Prep time: 45 minutes
Bake time: 45–55 minutes
Chill time: 2 hours
Makes: 16

120g unsalted butter, softened, plus extra for greasing
150g soft light brown sugar
25ml milk
1 tsp vanilla extract
185g plain flour
¼ tsp salt
100g dark chocolate chips

FOR THE FILLING
20 cookies and cream biscuits (I use Oreo)

FOR THE BROWNIE LAYER
235g dark chocolate
165g unsalted butter
2 large eggs
165g soft light brown sugar
1 tsp vanilla extract
65g plain flour
20g cocoa powder

Preheat the oven to 160°C fan/Gas Mark 4 and line a 20cm square tin with baking paper, greasing it with a little butter first to help the paper stick to it.

To make the cookie dough base, use a stand mixer with the paddle attachment for the best results. Mix the butter and sugar together for about 3 minutes until fluffy and well combined. Mix in the milk and vanilla extract until combined. Add the flour and salt and mix until a dough forms. Mix in the chocolate chips until well distributed. Press the cookie dough into the bottom of the tin in an even layer, using your fingertips or the back of a spoon. Chill in the fridge while you make the brownies, or for at least 30 minutes.

To make the brownie batter, melt the dark chocolate and butter together in a pan on a low heat. When fully melted, stir together and remove from the heat. Leave to cool for 5–10 minutes. In a mixing bowl, whisk together the eggs, sugar and vanilla extract with an electric hand mixer, or in a stand mixer with the whisk attachment for 5 minutes (set a timer for accuracy). Add the melted chocolate mixture, whisking constantly as you pour it in Gently mix in the flour and cocoa powder.

Recipe continues overleaf

Cover the cookie dough with the cookies and cream biscuits – you may need to chop some of the biscuits in half or quarters to fully cover the cookie dough and fill in any gaps. Pour the brownie batter over the top and smooth it out.

Bake for 45–55 minutes, the brownie layer should not wobble (or only very slightly) when you gently shake the tin. A cocktail stick or thin skewer inserted into the centre should come out with moist crumbs on it, but not be wet. Leave to cool completely in the tin, then chill in the fridge for 2 hours. To serve, remove from the tin and slice into squares using a sharp knife. Store in an airtight container in a cool place and eat within 3 days.

Traybakes

Cinnamon Rolls

Cinnamon rolls are the ultimate indulgence for weekend breakfasts and brunches, or a mid-morning snack any day of the week. These sweet, fragrant bread rolls are stuffed with cinnamon and brown sugar and topped with a sticky cream cheese glaze that is so good you may want to eat it with a spoon! They're soft and fluffy inside and gorgeously golden on the outside, this is a recipe you'll want to make again and again.

Prep time: 25 minutes
Proving time: 2 hours
Bake time: 25–30 minutes
Makes: 12

550g strong white bread flour, plus extra for dusting
1 sachet of fast-action yeast (7g)
¼ tsp salt
4 tbsp caster sugar
285ml semi-skimmed milk
75g unsalted butter
1 tsp vanilla extract
1 large egg
Vegetable oil, for greasing

FOR THE FILLING
150g soft light brown sugar
3 tsp ground cinnamon
30g unsalted butter, melted

FOR THE GLAZE
75g full-fat cream cheese
150g icing sugar
2 tbsp semi-skimmed milk

Put the flour, yeast, salt and sugar in a large bowl. Make sure not to pour the salt on top of the yeast, and vice versa, as in high concentrations salt can kill the yeast. Stir together – once the salt and yeast are evenly distributed throughout the mixture, the salt won't impact the yeast.

In a pan on a low heat, warm the milk and butter until the butter has melted, then add the vanilla extract. Leave to cool for 5 minutes or until lukewarm, then whisk in the egg. Pour into the flour mixture and bring everything together into a sticky dough. Knead the dough for 10 minutes, either by hand on a floured work surface or in a stand mixer with the dough hook attachment. Place the dough in a bowl that's been lightly brushed with vegetable oil, cover it with clingfilm or a clean tea towel and leave in a warm place to rise for 1 hour or until doubled in size.

While the dough is proving, make the cinnamon sugar filling by mixing the sugar with the cinnamon.

Roll out the dough into a rectangle measuring roughly 40 x 30cm. Brush the melted butter all over it, then sprinkle on the cinnamon sugar. Roll the dough into a sausage shape from the longest side, then use a sharp knife to trim the ends and cut it into 12 equal pieces.

Recipe continues overleaf

Traybakes

You can mark out the pieces before you cut with a ruler, you want them about 3–4cm thick. Place the rolls into a lined traybake tin (I used a 30 x 23cm one), cover them loosely with clingfilm or a clean tea towel and leave them to rise for 1 hour.

Preheat the oven to 180°C fan/Gas Mark 6.

Bake the rolls for 20–25 minutes until golden brown. Leave to cool.

To make the glaze, mix together the cream cheese, icing sugar and milk, and drizzle it over the rolls. Serve immediately. Store any leftovers in an airtight container in the fridge (or a cool place if they haven't been frosted) for up to 2 days.

SERTS

S'mores Baked Donuts

S'mores are an easy dessert made up of marshmallows and chocolate, sandwiched inside two biscuits, and heated so the chocolate melts and the marshmallows toast. I've turned these American campfire favourites into delicious baked donuts. This version has a super moist chocolate sponge, a rich chocolate ganache, toasted marshmallow topping and biscuit crumbs. You'll definitely be asking for some more!

Prep time: 30 minutes
Bake time: 12 minutes
Decorating time: 30 minutes
Makes: 12

Butter or baking spread, for greasing
100g caster sugar
75g soft light brown sugar
75g natural yoghurt
100ml milk
30ml vegetable oil
2 large eggs
200g self-raising flour
25g cocoa powder

FOR THE GLAZE
125g dark chocolate
85ml double cream
15g unsalted butter

FOR DECORATION
Mini marshmallows (gelatine-free if serving to vegetarians)
1 digestive biscuit, crushed

Preheat the oven to 160°C fan/Gas Mark 4 and grease two 6-hole donut tins with butter or baking spread.

In a mixing bowl, whisk together the caster sugar, brown sugar, yoghurt, milk, vegetable oil and eggs with a whisk. Add the flour and cocoa powder and whisk in until smooth. Divide the batter between the tins. You can put the batter into a piping bag or a jug to make it a bit easier to dispense into the trays, but you can use a spoon too. Bake for 12 minutes, then remove the donuts from the tin (I use a spoon to gently prise them out) and leave to cool on a wire rack.

To make the glaze, melt the dark chocolate and double cream together in a heatproof bowl in the microwave or over a pan of simmering water. Then add the butter and stir it in. Set the donuts onto a rack with a baking tray or some baking paper underneath to catch any drips. Dip the top and more rounded half of the donuts into the melted chocolate mixture and place back on the rack, un-iced side down.

Put the mini marshmallows on a plate and use a kitchen blowtorch to toast them. Alternatively, you can do this under a grill but keep a very close eye on them. Add the marshmallows to the donuts and sprinkle over the biscuit crumbs while the glaze is still wet. Store the donuts in an airtight container and eat within 3 days.

Chocolate Hazelnut Freakshake

When it comes to freakshakes, more is more! A delicious thick chocolate hazelnut milkshake is decorated and garnished like a childhood dream come true. There's whipped cream, chocolate hazelnut wafer bars, lashings of chocolate hazelnut spread and roasted hazelnut pieces. Grab a straw and tuck into this milkshake masterpiece.

Prep time: 20 minutes
Decorating time: 10 minutes
Serves: 2

200ml whole milk
100g chocolate hazelnut spread (I use Nutella)
300g vanilla or chocolate ice cream

FOR DECORATION
75g chocolate hazelnut spread (I use Nutella)
2 chocolate hazelnut wafer bars (I use Kinder Buenos)
2 milk chocolate bars (I use Kinder chocolate)
2 tbsp roasted hazelnuts, chopped
300ml double cream
1 tsp vanilla extract
1 tbsp icing sugar
25g chocolate sauce (I use Askeys)
2 chocolate fudge wafers

Use a butter knife to smear some of the chocolate hazelnut spread around the rims of two milkshake glasses (mine 'held' 300ml). Then stick some of the chocolate hazelnut wafer bar pieces and some of the milk chocolate bars into the chocolate hazelnut spread. Sprinkle the chopped hazelnuts over the chocolate hazelnut spread, filling in all the gaps between the chocolates. Chill the glasses in the fridge while you prepare the milkshake.

Place the milk, chocolate hazelnut spread and ice cream into a blender and blitz until fully combined. Alternatively, put in a jug and blitz with a stick blender.

In a mixing bowl, whip the double cream, vanilla extract and icing sugar with an electric hand whisk (or a hand whisk and a strong arm!) until thick and it holds its shape. Transfer it into a piping bag fitted with a nozzle of your choice. Drizzle the chocolate sauce onto the inside of the milkshake glasses, then divide the milkshake mixture between them, leaving about 1–2cm of space at the top for the toppings. Pipe the whipped cream on top of the milkshake. Decorate with the chocolate fudge wafers and the remaining chocolate hazelnut wafer bars and milk chocolate.

Warm the remaining chocolate hazelnut spread in a heatproof bowl in the microwave for 20–30 seconds, then drizzle over the freakshakes. Add straws and serve immediately.

Cherry Bakewell Pop Tarts

Pop tarts bring back memories of childhood, I remember enjoying this rare and coveted breakfast treat, that always had a molten hot centre! This homemade version is so much better than the shop-bought American favourite, the pastry is buttery and crisp, the filling plentiful and the decoration a delight. The cherry and almond flavours of Bakewell shine through in every element of these tasty pastry treats!

Prep time: 45 minutes
Chill time: 50 minutes
Bake time: 20 minutes
Decorating time: 15 minutes
Makes: 5

200g plain flour, plus extra for dusting
100g ground almonds
1 tbsp caster sugar
135g unsalted butter, cold
1 large egg, plus 1 for the glaze
1 tbsp milk

FOR THE FILLING
1 tsp cornflour
135g cherry jam

FOR DECORATION
125g icing sugar
1 tsp almond extract
1–1½ tbsp milk
15 glacé cherries, halved
1 tbsp flaked almonds

To make the pastry, put the flour, ground almonds and sugar into a mixing bowl, or the bowl of a food processor, and mix together. Add the butter in small cubes, or you can also grate it into the flour mixture. Rub in the butter using your fingertips, or if using a food processor pulse, until the mixture resembles fine breadcrumbs. Add the egg and milk and mix until the pastry starts to clump together. Press the pastry into a flattened square and wrap it tightly in clingfilm. Chill in the fridge for 30 minutes.

While the pastry is chilling, make the filling. Mix the cornflour and jam together and set aside.

Remove the pastry from the fridge and remove the clingfilm. On a work surface dusted with flour, roll out the pastry into a rectangle measuring roughly 25 x 37cm. Trim the edges so you have a rectangle with straight sides, then cut out ten rectangles measuring 11 x 7cm.

Put five of the rectangles onto a lined baking tray, then spoon the jam into the middle of each one, leaving a gap of roughly 1cm around the edge. Crack the egg for the glaze into a bowl and beat it with a fork. Brush the beaten egg along the 1cm gaps around the edges of each jam-covered pastry rectangle. Sandwich the remaining pastry rectangles over the jam-covered ones, and gently press down the edges to seal them.

Recipe continues overleaf

Desserts

Go over the edges with the tip of a fork, gently pressing it all around to leave little indents. Use a cocktail stick to poke a few holes in the top of each pastry to let steam escape during baking. Chill the pop tarts in the fridge for 20 minutes.

Meanwhile, preheat the oven to 180°C fan/Gas Mark 6.

Brush more of the beaten egg all over the pop tarts, then bake for 20 minutes, or until golden all over. Leave to cool completely.

To decorate, mix the icing sugar, almond extract and milk together. Add the milk slowly as you may not need it all. You are aiming for a thick but spreadable consistency. Spread the icing over the pop tarts, then decorate each one with three glacé cherry halves and some flaked almonds while the icing is still wet. Leave to set. Store any leftovers in an airtight container in a cool place and eat within 3 days.

TIP

If you're in a hurry, you can use shop-bought shortcrust pastry for this recipe.

Battenberg Swiss Roll

Despite its German name, Battenberg is a very British creation and marzipan lovers have ensured that it has stood the test of time. This Battenberg Swiss roll has a filling of apricot jam and soft whipped cream. On top are mini versions of Battenberg (but don't worry they're shop-bought!). This cute and colourful Swiss roll makes such a pretty centrepiece on your table.

Prep time: 30 minutes
Bake time: 12 minutes
Decorating time: 25 minutes
Serves: 12

Butter or baking spread, for greasing
4 large eggs
100g caster sugar
1 tsp almond extract
Yellow food colouring
Pink food colouring
75g plain flour
25g ground almonds

FOR THE FILLING
250ml double cream
1 tsp vanilla extract
1 tbsp icing sugar
100g apricot jam

FOR DECORATION
2 mini Battenberg cakes (I use Mr Kipling)

Preheat the oven to 160°C fan/Gas Mark 4 and line a Swiss roll tin or a baking tray with a lip with baking paper (the one I used measures 38.5 x 25.5 x 2.2cm). Use a little butter or baking spread to help the baking paper stick to the tray.

For the sponge, whisk the eggs and sugar together with an electric hand whisk or in a stand mixer with the whisk attachment for 8 minutes until it reaches ribbon stage. This is when the mixture is pale, thick and has doubled in size, and you can drizzle some of the mixture into itself in a figure of eight and it takes at least 3 seconds to sink back in. Add the almond extract and whisk a little to mix it in.

Divide the mixture equally between two mixing bowls (or leave half in your stand mixer and put half in a separate mixing bowl). Add the yellow food colouring to one bowl and whisk it in using an electric hand whisk or stand mixer with the whisk attachment. Add the pink food colouring to the other bowl and whisk it in again using an electric hand whisk or stand mixer with the whisk attachment.

In a smaller bowl, stir the flour and ground almonds together. Then split the mixture in half so you have two lots of 50g.

Fold half of the flour and almond mixture into the bowl of yellow batter, then fold the other half into the bowl of pink batter. Fold them in slowly and carefully with a spatula or spoon until fully combined.

Desserts

Recipe continues overleaf

Transfer each of the batter mixtures into their own piping bag, snip off the ends with scissors or use round piping nozzles. Pipe the batter into the tin in alternate colours widthways, so that you have a striped effect. If you have any batter left, go over the corresponding coloured stripes again until it's all used up. Bake for 12 minutes, and while it is baking lay a clean sheet of baking paper out on your work surface. Remove the sponge from the oven and immediately tip it out onto the baking paper. Remove the baking paper the sponge was baked with, place another clean piece of baking paper over it and flip the sponge over, remove the baking paper covering the top and roll up the sponge, starting from one of the shorter ends and taking the clean baking paper underneath with it. Transfer to a wire rack to cool completely. You can place a small glass or cup on either side of it to stop it from unrolling if needed.

For the filling, place the cream, vanilla extract and icing sugar into a mixing bowl. Use an electric hand whisk, or stand mixer with the whisk attachment, to whip it up until it is thick and holds its shape. Gently unroll the sponge and spread the apricot jam all over it, then spread a layer of the whipped cream over the jam. If you want to decorate the top of the sponge with whipped cream, then make sure to save some of it. Re-roll the sponge and place onto a serving plate. If you like, pipe some whipped cream on top and decorate with sliced mini Battenbergs. Serve immediately and store any leftovers in the fridge for up to 2 days.

TIP
Instead of mini Battenbergs, you could decorate the Swiss roll with some flaked almonds or roll some golden marzipan into little balls.

Desserts

Pancake Cereal

Pancake cereal is the viral breakfast creation that took the internet by storm. It combines two breakfast favourites into one extra cute bowlful of deliciousness. These tiny pancakes are easy to make using a squeezy bottle or a piping bag. Kids and big kids alike will be charmed by their adorable appearance. The only decision you'll need to make is whether to add milk or maple syrup!

Prep time: 30 minutes
Cook time: 15–20 minutes
Serves: 2–4 depending on hunger levels

50g unsalted butter
145g plain flour
1½ tsp baking powder
40g caster sugar
Pinch of salt
200ml milk
1 large egg
1 tsp vanilla extract
    (optional)

TO SERVE
Maple syrup
Fresh fruit
Milk of your choice

Put a large frying pan on a medium heat. Place the butter into a heatproof bowl and microwave in 10-second blasts, stirring between each one, until fully melted. It will take 30–40 seconds in a 900W microwave, or you can melt it in a pan on a low heat.

In a mixing bowl, stir together the flour, baking powder, sugar and salt. In a large jug, or another mixing bowl, whisk together the milk, egg and vanilla extract (if using). Next, whisk in the melted butter. Pour the milk mixture into the flour mixture and whisk to combine into a smooth batter.

Transfer the batter into a squeezy bottle, or a piping bag. Add small blobs of the pancake batter to the frying pan, covering as much of the frying pan's surface as you can. Cook the mini pancakes for 1–2 minutes until golden on the underside, then flip over and cook the other side for about 1 minute. Set on a cooling rack. Repeat with the remaining batter

Divide the mini pancakes between cereal bowls and serve immediately with your choice of toppings.

Bronuts

What do you get when you cross a brownie with a donut? A bronut! If you're a fan of the edge pieces in a batch of brownies, then this is the dessert for you. Rich chocolatey brownie batter is baked in a ring-shaped donut mould. With each mouthful you'll get a crunchy brownie edge, as well as some fudgy middle. Even better, they're smothered in creamy milk chocolate and decorated with even more chocolatey goodies and sprinkles.

Prep time: 30 minutes
Bake time: 12–15 minutes
Decorating time: 30 minutes
Makes: 12

Cake release spray or vegetable oil, for greasing
235g dark chocolate
165g unsalted butter
2 large eggs
165g soft light brown sugar
1 tsp vanilla extract
80g plain flour

FOR DECORATION
200g milk chocolate
25g white chocolate
Various sprinkles and chocolates of your choice

Preheat the oven to 160°C fan/Gas Mark 4 and spray two 6-hole silicone donut moulds with cake release spray, or brush with some vegetable oil.

Melt the dark chocolate and butter together in a pan on a low heat, stirring occasionally. When fully melted, remove from the heat. Leave to cool for 5 minutes.

In a mixing bowl using an electric hand mixer, or in the bowl of a stand mixer with the whisk attachment, whisk together the eggs, sugar and vanilla extract for exactly 5 minutes (set a timer for accuracy) until thicker and paler in colour. Slowly add the chocolate and butter mixture, whisking constantly as you pour it in. Gently whisk in the flour. Transfer the mixture into a piping bag or a jug and divide it equally between the donut rings. Bake for 12–15 minutes, depending on how crispy you like the edge. Leave to cool completely in the moulds.

Place the bronuts on a sheet of baking paper on a work surface ready for decorating. Melt the chocolate in a heatproof bowl in the microwave (blast for 30 seconds, stir, then blast in 10-second intervals, stirring between each one) or over a pan of simmering water. Dip the more rounded half of the bronuts into the melted chocolate, then place back on to the baking paper. Melt the white chocolate in the same way and drizzle it over the bronuts.

Desserts

Recipe continues overleaf

Add your sprinkles, chocolates and other decorations while the chocolate is still wet so that they stick. Leave the chocolate to set fully. Store in an airtight container in a cool place and eat within 3 days.

TIP
You can dip the bronuts in white or dark chocolate if you prefer and customise the decoration to your favourite flavours.

Red Velvet Cake Truffles

If there's one thing that I'm certain of, it's that red velvet cake and cream cheese belong together! These cake truffles combine bright and moist red velvet cake with cream cheese to create a rich and very moreish treat. They're dipped in white chocolate and decorated with a fun drizzle of red chocolate. The great thing about this recipe is you can make it with any leftover cake, so it's even easier if you're in a rush.

Prep time: 45 minutes
Bake time: 20–25 minutes
Chill time: 1 hour
Decorating time: 30 minutes
Makes: 30

150g baking spread, softened, plus extra for greasing
150g caster sugar
2 large eggs
1 tsp vanilla extract
1½ tbsp cocoa powder
½ tsp bicarbonate of soda
½ tsp red food colouring (I use Sugarflair red extra)
85ml buttermilk
165g self-raising flour
300g full-fat cream cheese

FOR DECORATION
400g white chocolate (milk and dark chocolate can be used if you prefer)
50g red candy melts (optional)

Preheat the oven to 160°C fan/Gas Mark 4 and line a cupcake tin with cupcake cases, or grease and line a 20cm cake tin at least 5cm deep.

Mix the baking spread and sugar together until fluffy, ideally with an electric mixer for about 3 minutes. Mix in the eggs and vanilla extract. Gently whisk in the cocoa powder, bicarbonate of soda, red food colouring, buttermilk and flour until fully combined. Divide the mixture evenly between the cupcake cases or spread out in an even layer in the cake tin.

Bake the cupcakes for 20–25 minutes or until a skewer inserted into the centre of the cupcakes comes out clean. Bake the cake for 30–35 minutes or until a skewer inserted into the centre comes out clean. Leave to cool completely.

Tip the cupcakes or cake into a large mixing bowl (removing the paper cases from the cupcakes) and use a fork or your hands to break it into fine crumbs. You can also do this in a food processor. Weigh your cake crumbs – you will need half the amount of cream cheese. My cake crumbs weighed 600g and I used 300g of cream cheese. Add the cream cheese to the cake crumbs and mix it in until well combined. You should be able to take chunks of the mixture out with your hands and press together into balls.

Recipe continues overleaf

Desserts

Roll the mixture into balls using your hands, weighing them so that they're all a similar size if you like – mine were 25g each. Place them onto a lined baking tray, then chill in the freezer for at least 1 hour.

To decorate, melt the chocolate in a heatproof bowl in the microwave (blast for 30 seconds, stir, then blast in 10-second intervals, stirring between each one) or over a pan of simmering water. Remove the cake truffles from the freezer and dip them into the chocolate, coating them fully. Use a fork to remove them from the chocolate and place them onto some baking paper to set. Melt the red candy melts, or you can use the same amount of white chocolate and colour it with red food colouring. Drizzle it over the truffles to decorate. Serve immediately. Store any leftovers in the fridge and eat within 5 days.

TIP

You can make this recipe with any cake or leftover cake cuttings, just weigh the cake and use half the amount of cream cheese.

Index

About the Author

Kat Buckley is a professional blogger living in Manchester, England. She has been blogging at The Baking Explorer for a decade, with a focus on sharing recipes and how to guides. She has been highly acclaimed by Vuelio, Feedspot and BritMums and her recipes have been featured in Baking Heaven magazine. Kat is passionate about making baking accessible to everyone and sharing the joy that food can bring.

Acknowledgements

The biggest thank you goes to my number one fan, my project manager and biggest supporter – my wonderful husband Lewis. I could not have created this book without you! You have been endlessly supportive and encouraging during the making of this book.

To my beautiful boy Enzo, you were too little to help me make this book (although you always wanted to), but you have been so sweet and understanding about mummy having to work more than usual to complete this project. I will love you forever and you are the best thing I ever made.

To all my friends and family, whether you were in the know about my secret project, or you had no idea. Thank you for your support, for checking in with me, for giving me second opinions, for understanding when I said I was "super busy with work" for several months, and for what I know you will do when the book comes out – shout about it far and wide!

Thank you to every single person that has ever visited my website, followed me on social media, and most of all made my recipes! It all adds up and it helps The Baking Explorer grow. You are all such a huge part of this book, and I am so excited to see you make and enjoy the recipes inside.

And finally thank you so much to my publishers for supporting me throughout this project and giving me this amazing opportunity!

Acknowledgements

1

Pop Press, an imprint of Ebury Publishing,
20 Vauxhall Bridge Road,
London, SW1V 2SA

Pop Press is part of the Penguin Random House group of companies
whose addresses can be found at global.penguinrandomhouse.com

Penguin
Random House
UK

Copyright © Kat Buckley 2023
Photography © Kat Buckley 2023
Design by Studio Polka

Kat Buckley has asserted its right to be identified as the author of this Work
in accordance with the Copyright, Designs and Patents Act 1988

First published by Pop Press in 2023

www.penguin.co.uk

A CIP catalogue record for this book is available from the British Library

ISBN: 9781529905335

Printed and bound in China by C & C Offset Printing Co., Ltd

The authorised representative in the EEA is Penguin Random House Ireland,
Morrison Chambers, 32 Nassau Street, Dublin D02 YH68.

Penguin Random House is committed to a sustainable future for our
business, our readers and our planet. This book is made from Forest
Stewardship Council® certified paper.

MIX
Paper | Supporting
responsible forestry
FSC® C018179